Introduction to Destruction & Hope

Each year, many people are injured or lose their lives in house fires. Most understand how truly destructive fire can be. If you are fortunate enough never to have experienced one yourself, you almost certainly know someone who has.

Perhaps it is not surprising that I was unable to find a global statistic; however, in the United States, "approximately 344,600 house fires occur annually, according to Guardian Service" (Lewis, D., reviewed by Credle, K., 2025).

Roughly, this equates to about 944 house fires a day in the United Kingdom, or around 34,000 per year. According to a recent blog post by Morgan Clark, "across Great Britain, house fires occur at a rate of 498 fires per one million people" (Morgan Clark, 2024).

Litter Bug Embers

At the beginning of the poem, the mention of growing plants in open spaces creates a peaceful setting; however, litterbugs leave rubbish in the sunlight, which can ignite embers and flames.

This contrast prompts readers to recognise the risks posed by wildfires when people fail to dispose of litter responsibly.

The imagery serves as a stark reminder that food wrappers, glass bottles, and picnic remnants can become fuel in a dry, natural environment. The powerful consequences of human actions— even those that seem insignificant—can be devastating.

Something as innocent as a picnic or a night of camping in a national park is often marred by human negligence: the simple act of forgetting to respect nature.

The setting is described as both majestic and tragic, shaped by human neglect. The wildfire, born of carelessness, devastates the landscape's natural beauty. Yet, the element of fire also plays a vital role within ecosystems — clearing away dead material and, for particular plant species, releasing essential nutrients. These effects can be positive; however, "wildfires are frequently caused by human actions, either deliberate or accidental" (AI Overview: Google, 2024).

On a more positive note, fire can symbolise change and renewal. As tragic as a blaze may be, it often marks the beginning of new growth — a chance for life to start again.

This duality echoes the symbolism found in some of the world's oldest monotheistic religions, such as **Zoroastrianism**, founded more than 3,000 years ago (Zinna, A., 2023).

Azerbaijan holds a deep connection to fire — so much so that it is known as the *Land of Fire*. According to a *BBC Travel* article, the nation's economic development has long been fuelled by its vast reserves of natural gas and oil, both of which are key to its identity and progress.

When relating fire to Greek mythology, one need look no further than Hephaestus - the God of the forge. He used the flames as a source of creativity, even while carrying a heart scarred by revenge after his mother cast him into the ocean as a child.

 It was common for him to be covered in soot and ash from his furnace, tirelessly crafting exquisite objects: jewellery, adornments for the gods, and the legendary armour of Achilles.

Hephaestus is celebrated as the foremost divine blacksmith - his symbols, fittingly, are the anvil, hammer, and pliers.

Hephaestus

The poem "Hephaestus" is a myth-inspired narrative that explores resilience, transformation, and divine craftsmanship. It weaves vivid imagery and symbolism to interpret themes of abandonment, revenge, and redemption. The tragedy of a discarded child becomes a story of power reclaimed — a journey from rejection to creation, where fire no longer destroys, but forges destiny.

The presentation of **Hephaestus** portrays him as both a mythological figure and a symbol of endurance, dignity, and creation.
 Through the flames of fire, his story forms a narrative arc of cruelty and imperfection — a tale that burns yet rebuilds.

This portrayal humanises the Greek gods, aligning them with earthly occupations such as blacksmiths and welders — those who labour beside the furnace, shaping the raw into the remarkable. It pays homage to generations of working-class artisans who have spent long hours in the heat, bringing metal to life.

By referencing his creations — adornments and battle armour — the poem reveals the beauty that can exist within a destructive force: the act of turning trauma and pain into art.
 A divine echo of creative therapy —forging healing through creation.

Resilience is born from rejection, and fire is a powerful symbol of renewal. Positive change is ultimately achieved through hard work and perseverance. An abandoned baby becomes a god, like a phoenix rising from the ashes. He is the god of fire and the "master craftsman, master of fire, and master of forging" (Blakeley, 2023).

The Roman equivalent of *Hephaestus* is *Vulcan.* Despite his excellent skills in handicraft and mental work, Vulcan was nevertheless perceived as ugly. He is known as "the Roman God of fire and forge" (Apel, T., 2022). This contrast leads to an interesting question: Why was Vulcan considered ugly?

Why the Ugliest Gods?

After exploring Vulcan's story, I was inspired to write the following poems in response to the information I read. Suppose Vulcan were a man living in the 21st century. In that case, society in general might not discriminate against him, though some individuals would still display cruelty, much like Juno, Vulcan's mother and queen of the Gods. This reflects societal attitudes of the late nineteenth and early twentieth centuries, when "legislation, administered by Commissioners in Lunacy, was dominant[...]no clear distinction between learning disability and mental illness" (The Open University, 2025). The article includes a disclaimer that references to lunacy, now considered highly offensive, are rejected by the university.

However, progress remains incomplete. Recent statistics (2024) indicate that "disabled people experience widespread discrimination[...]with high rates of negative attitudes and behaviours reported" (AI Overview, 2025). To ensure a truly inclusive society, urgent action must be taken to address and dismantle these persistent barriers.

Lights Whilst Travelling

While I am not particularly familiar with this year's seasonal events, the announcement of Long Leat's Summer Carnival and the inclusion of British icons in The Festival of Light (featuring Wallace & Gromit and friends) inspired me to write another poem.

Although I have not visited *Long Leat,* reading the advertisement for its festive celebrations evoked memories of family car journeys to London for theatre performances or to visit relatives. We would set out at lunchtime and return in the evening, captivated by the city's dazzling lights. London's Christmas illuminations are truly unforgettable, typically switched on in early November and remaining lit until around January 5th, according to Londonist. The Trafalgar Square Christmas tree lights, however, are usually illuminated in early December (Reynolds, L., 2025).

This period is longer than the average pantomime season, but comparable to the festive season at *Long* Leat's Festival of Light. The event is promoted as an opportunity to "make it a Christmas to remember at the Festival of Light on selected dates from 8 November 2025 – 11 January 2026" (Long Leat, 2025).

Place

Writing the following poem introduced me to the concept of the hearth, or hearth fire, within a religious context, even referencing hearth fire cults. Uda Becker describes the hearth fire as "a house of community, warmth and safety, of family, and of women" (Becker, U., 2000), presenting it as a powerful religious symbol of fire.

In modern terms, I associate the hearth fire with the concept of girl power, as embodied by the pop group the *Spice Girls*—the strength and sense of community that women and girls share. Marissa Johnson, reflecting on the era when the Spice Girls' single "Wannabe" topped the charts, describes the group as "a phenomenon, and their Girl Power mantra was impossible to escape [...] songs like You Don't Own Me and I Am a Woman served as anthems for the second wave of feminism in the 60s and 70s" (Johnson, M., 2021). The two songs Johnson mentions suggest that they embody the spirit of the hearth fire.

It is essential to acknowledge that, based on my limited research, some of this information may be outdated.

Becker's book, for instance, was published twenty-five years ago. The tradition of honouring ancestors and spirits—often by making offerings and keeping the fire burning continuously—underscores the enduring significance of the hearth (Aburrow, Y., 2016). Nevertheless, these insights proved to be an intriguing source of inspiration.

Fire Still Speaks

The conclusion of the poem serves as a warning: even after the visible flames have faded, we must not overlook the lingering embers. Fire is depicted as a small idea that can create a deceptive sense of safety. Although fire may start small, harmless, and almost invisible, it can quickly grow and intensify. As the destruction escalates, this progression underscores the importance of remaining vigilant against embers and other potential hazards. The East District Council, for example, has legislation prohibiting the lighting of bonfires when wind may carry smoke or burning embers onto neighbouring properties (East District Council, 2023).

The Knowledge that Grows

New life experiences are shaped by the decisions we make and the consequences that follow. Each choice paves the way for a new adventure. As one spiritual blog describes: "when we hold onto the light of discovery, taking the novelty of a thing full circle, we grow as a person" (Henry, A., 2021). When I wrote the poem "*The Knowledge that Grows*," *my motivation* was not spiritual reflection, but rather an exploration of our fundamental drive for survival as human beings. This concept resonates with the music and lyrics of Sir Elton John and Tim Rice's "Circle of Life" from The Lion King.

"It's the circle of life.

And it moves us all.

Through despair and hope.

And it moves us all.

Through despair and hope.

Through faith and love.

Till we faith and love.

Till we find our place.

On the path unwinding.

In the circle,

The circle of life" (Genius, 1994).

Burning Destruction

Litter Bug Embers

Growing plants
in open spaces.
Majestic beauty—
a tragic event.
It begins with
the leftovers
of a picnic.
Litter becomes fuel
for burning embers.

Rapid Flames

Smouldering forever—
 remains the scene
 of an unexpected fire.

Burning nature's beauty.
With not a care in the world
for the harm to come.

Destruction leaping,
from spark to spark

The House Fire

I never, ever thought—
my family home
would suddenly start burning.

A routine,
smoke alarm check—
That's what I thought,
When I heard
The echoes of danger.

The sight of flames,
the smell that lingers
right through your veins.

The five senses—
They are exploring.
The smell—
of smoke.
It is choking.

Flashback: Charring or Freezing

A sacrifice.
The need
to escape.

Levels of destruction—
just as cruel
as an ice age.

The weight of hate
equals
uncontrollable flames.

The Ember Witch

The ember witch—
in a fire's grip,
writing spells
born of emotion.

A trembling lip,
a potion
mixes.

Ember witches live life and death,
in between each other.

No one dares cross them,
and their magic.
Molten lava.
Runs through,
their thoughts and feelings.

The ember witches,
their voices
scorch the landscape.

Walking straight through
the molten mist,
You have truly witnessed
the ember witch's magic.

A Suspect in Smoke

Witnessing
the sparks and flames,
the distant glow—
far,
far away.

The dread,
sucking the life
out of
the window frame.

Whispers and shouts
cross each other out.
An explanation
of life—
 extinguished.

People frozen.
The smoke
swallows
everybody's words.

Dreams & Nightmares (By the Fire)

In that place where magic gleams,
The flame becomes the judge
of all your dreams.

Fire turning—
Its wrath upon you.
Once again.

Falter once,
and the nightmares arrive.
The fire consumes
all that is good
and all that is bad.

Eruption

A sleeping sound
beneath the rock and stone.

Carvings in ashes—
leaving nothing
But bones.

Blood running,
the shade
Of pure red.
Lava stirring
Inside a rock's head.

Warnings in the smoke,
spotted in the distance.
Crowns of sparks grow brighter,
turning to embers.

Fire's Deceit

Fire kissing the salty sea.
A chance
It might set the world free.

The furnace heart beating forever,
Steady in its place.
A burning glow was seen.
Further afield.

The power sleeps,
but doesn't admit defeat.
A burning demise,
It never dies.
A dark disguise.

Damage & Healing Ice & Fire

Rumours say the world will end
by fire -
too much war.
Too much warming.

Fire swallowing,
Absolutely everything -
through the bone.
Through the flesh,
Of humans and animals.

An icy wind,
torn apart -
by bright, red flames.

A rageful,
angry parent -
beginning to heal.
The flames become
charred ashes.
Soon,
The rain thunders.

Early morning frosts return -
again and again.
Soon,
the drops reappear.
Turning them -
into icicles.

Fears of Fireworks

Foxes flinch,
as owls retreat.
Deer stand.
Frozen to the spot.

A thousand sparks
Turn the sky -
silver, red, and gold.

The dread -
the fear within the forest.
Blooms of fire
reappears -
in flashes.

As quickly
as the fireworks started.
Works of art disappear -
Rather suddenly.

Screaming Stars

Screaming stars, so far away.
Glass cracking,
It's heard for miles.
On a particular day.

Each screaming star
makes the moon shine strongly.
Each shard of glass,
Falls.
Flies.
Causing severe damage beautifully.

If it comes towards you,
Stand back.
Take cover.

The screaming stars.
They are shards of glass.
Travelling -
because of a fire.

Fire on Rampage

Once the fire
was extinguished -
Now, it doesn't obey.

Leaping sparkles.
Leaping amber.
Leaping embers.

Still leaving scars,
a punch to the heart.
That's how fire
does its damage.

A Fire's Walk

Dressed in a coloured gown,
strolling down the streets.

Buildings collapse,
falling straight to the ground.

Sparks break away,
Kissing the path.
As fire.
As flames.
It begins its rampage.

Factory Sparks

Early mornings,
late, late nights.

A warehouse.
A production line.

Factory mechanisms -
sparks start flying.
Working -
just as hard.
As the employees.
Hard at work,
inside the warehouse.

The building screams -
With growing heat.
Sirens wait,
echoing left and right.

Fire's Crime & Trial

Silence ruled the forest.
Leaves and branches
crashed to the ground -
As the birds began to panic.
The fire's flames -
They are the judge and jury.
Roots and flowers
become victims.
Burning to ashes.
Steams do their best
to defend the forest,
while flames lick
the tree trunks.

Lighter

A child playing
in the street.

Teenagers nearby
mess around -
with a lighter.
Also,
Trying to buy
cigarettes.

The lighter strikes a flame -
a moment
of mesmerisation.

It drops.
The flames grin
Making contact with the grass.
That's been deprived of a drink.

Forgotten Name

It is a hungry patient.
Fire, like time,
erases the past.
Even scares ghosts
in chimneys -
Reaching higher,
and higher.
A town once stood,
when the sun rose.
By dusk,
overlooking hills -
whispering the forgotten name.

Wiping Memories of Destruction

What did the fire do best?
Sparks and embers -
swallowing the memories
of a woodland picnic.

Roots and flowers
become the victims.
The fire's flames
Pronounce the wood -
Guilty!

Sentencing nature to death -
by burning.
The animals and the woodland
suffer deeply.

Not so Hopeful

Hopeful in fire's presence -
an inner power,
an outer layer of destruction.

The triumphant -
They are successful.
Those who fail
Stand at the edge of evil,
Jumping into darkness.

Not all embers
These are signs of hopefulness.
These paths
are blindingly bright;
nevertheless,
Light is not always positive.

The sharp edges of doubt
can bring a strange joy -
or likely, despair -
the feeling of falling.

Running Away from the Blaze

Echoing laughter -
a sonic boom impacts,
Leaving a small town
in complete chaos.

The wildfire,
always wins best dressed
at a beauty competition.

A gift -
Zero congratulations.
Embers plan a party,
and you
are invited.

PSD of a Blaze

Each night at this time -
the second week in January -
The mind comes alive.

Like the flame of a candle,
a reminder of a tale
That equals disaster.

Wax burning,
The mind is returning.

Many lives lost.
The guilt, again,
is rising.

A respectful silence -
Zero progression.
The fight for justice
forgotten.

The struggle.
The memory.
The past and present.

Videos, photographs,
and newspapers -
images glued,
staying with survivors.

No Mood for a Party

A five-day celebration.
A new year begins.
A festival of lights
marks the calendar -
The month of the lunar.

When fire sends bangs and cracks,
explodes unexpectedly,
extremely close
to local buildings,

Two drivers,
driving at speed.
A scooter joins the traffic,
carrying supplies
for the festival of Diwali.

Who could have known
Three people would meet,
followed by a fireball -
a sudden,
unexpected tragedy.
Now, no one
is in the mood for a party.

Fire Still Speaks

Listening to embers,
releasing sparks of communication.
Witnesses weep
at the sight of disaster.

Flames laugh
at desperate cries.
Little do the embers know -
names will be carved
into the night sky.

A chair of choking smoke,
singing
Final notes.
Yet an echoing grief
fills the absence
of moon and sun.

Walls once stood;
They are now only dust.
Echoing laughter follows
mysterious shadows,
writing and receiving
the darkest of letters.

Fallen Angel

Flames tore through brick and wood -
an arson attack
in a family home.

Some escape,
after climbing out a window.
Some make it out
onto a balcony,
as a neighbour
runs across the road with a ladder.

One year later,
The burns have faded,
But the scars remain.
The house
has disappeared
forever.

Twenty years on,
There's one less chair at the table.
A shadow haunts the family -
of a son
who never grew into a teenager,
and a Dad

who never saw the years
described as golden.

The two who are gone,
but not forgotten.
They have missed so much.
Still, no one knows
Why was the house a target?

The Haunted House

An empty shell of a house.
No one has lived there
since the Second World War.

The house was bombed
by the Blitz.
Sixty years later,
A removal van appears on the street.

A family,
new to the neighbourhood,
didn't know the history -
Or the bombing sixty years ago.

As furniture
begins to be moved inside,
doors and windows
open and close
all by themselves.
Ignored that evening.
Until -
creatures creep on the landing.

A local offers help -

Unusual for most.
They arrive on the doorstep
with sage and incense:
Cleansing, smudging.
How is this helping?

That night,
no creatures
appeared on the landing.

Igniting Hope

Magic of Fire

Spells are working,
bringing hope to the lonely.
The cauldron heats up
as the potion begins bubbling.
A magical change of location—
sparks of nervousness and excitement.
Plans so positive
finish with doubts now burning.
A spell cast in perfect motion;
Events can go wrong.
When they go right,
happiness bubbles, just like the potion.
With a puff of smoke,
The concoction burns,
following the wind
wherever it takes them.

Unexpected Flame

Lightning strikes.
Fire ignites.

The sun is high in the sky -
the biggest star
burns and shines,
rebuilding the damage.

The thoughts of the lightning
wiped away,
as another storm returns.

Residents state,
"We are more
prepared for the lightning
returning."

Fire Guide

Charming sights -
However, danger controls the smog
taking hold throughout the night.
By luck,
or by chance,
unfortunate events
turn to pure strength.

Everyone is coming closer
together much more often.
It could have happened
before the flames came knocking.
Regardless,
the fire's been a guide
to a better community.

Ashbird

Rumours of an ashbird
flying across the stars -
wings of fire
tearing clouds to pieces.

When a child is lost,
a match is lit
by the ashbird.
A tear-drop spark
lights the way for the child.

Returning home,
safe and sound.
The child was lost,
But the ashbird
helped the child be found.

Warm, Winter Welcome

Trees stand as the sun wakes.
Branches waving,
The very few leaves are dancing.

The sun rises,
fire glowing.
Winter frost
helps the sun glitter.

Blue skies,
But the air is freezing.
You return inside
after welcoming -
the start of winter.

The Old Man: Tears of Fire

An old man
sits beneath the cliffs,
sheltered by a cave.
His shaky hands
can still light a single match.

The cliff, at times,
shakes -
causing rocks to fall.
The older man's match
keeps him warm.

Still damp and shivering,
with cold,
the single flame remains -
the size of a teardrop.

Echoes and whispers.
The glow of the ember
creates a small path
of soot and ashes.

A man prefers the cave
as his abode.

He feels closer to the sea,
the seagulls and fish,
than to people.

A Warm Landscape

Trees stand as the sun wakes.
Branches waving,
The very few leaves are dancing.

The sun rises,
fire glowing.
Winter frost
helps the sun glitter.

Blue skies,
But the air is freezing.
You return inside
after welcoming -
the start of winter.

Finding the Fire

A frosty day where embers hide.
It takes a breath,
and the embers rise.

A down reflecting,
kind courage.
Through ice,
the sun restores -
the postcard picture.

As evening arrives,
clouds of grey
gather in the sky.

No storm steals the flames -
those are gone,
non-existent.

Small String of Hope

If it is doomed from the start,
The fire will embrace
your heart -
burning fiercely,
full of light,
beauty, and grace.
All the scars
will heal
after witnessing the lava's damage.
All the sorrow,
all the hurt -
beneath what's destroyed,
there is
a small string of hope.

Escape the Winter

Escaping the cold
for a warm reception.
Travelling to escape
winter's freezing temperatures,
with coldness melting upon arrival.

Witnessing the burning star
immediately brings a smile.
Planning the days
with a warmth -
deep within your veins.

The sight of the flame,
burning brightly,
almost every single day.

Jack-O'-Lantern Game

A pumpkin's soul,
glowing brightly.
The beacon allows screams
of "Trick-or-Treat!"
A jack-o'-lantern -
playing friendly games
Every year on Halloween,
The 31st of October.

Pumpkin Candles

Tiny flames -
not wild and out of control,
just a flicker
of a spark.

The light reveals
the pumpkin's creation.
The face glows,
thanks to the candle.

The playful pumpkin's
Its candle flame is inviting,
yet creepy all the same -
illuminating crooked teeth
as the orange vegetable
forces a smile.

A guide for children trick-or-treating,
The candle flame giggles
from right inside the pumpkin.
When the full moon
appears among the stars,
the pumpkin candles
are blown

Straight out.
Next morning,
The pumpkin candles are stored away,
awaiting to be set alight
for next October -
the recommencing
of Halloween games.

Heading to the Moon

Flying above our planet Earth,
sparks escape
from the rocket ship's engine.

Space skies
seem to accept
the ship and its crew.
The planets and stars
do the same too.

The engine is screaming
on the way to the moon.
It isn't made of cheese,
So the crew
are now
making their way home.

Rocket Smoke

Pines under the umbrella of night.
Excitement
of a rocket launch
all around the world.

Zero lightning bolts,
no matches in sight -
just deafening rumbles
as the countdown starts.

Sparks soon follow,
then a flood of smoke.
With one shot,
the rocket sets off.

Smoke still lingers.
The roars still ring
in the ears of witnesses.

Rocket Engine

Soaring past
the Earth and stars,
The rocket passes
Venus and Mars.

The farther astronauts travel,
The rocket engines keep burning -
It's a real struggle.

Passing Earth into the Milky Way,
Other planets are spotted:
Jupiter and Saturn.

Further travelling
through the solar system,
through the rocket's window,
sparks bounce away
in the stars -
space's ocean.

Fireworks Painting the Skies

Fireworks paint pictures
Every 5th of November.
From beginning
to the end,
Countless portraits are created.

Darker nights
fuel the sparklers -
artists' paint brushes,
embers of light
leaving shadows of people:
Young,
Old,
and teenagers.

Many a BANG!
Many a WOOSH!

Winter's arriving
as more colours
weave among the stars,
waving to the cow
jumping over the moon
in the nursery rhyme.

Camping

"We are going camping."
The children sing in chorus.
"A week's holiday,
camping in Hampshire."

Arriving at our destination,
we have to put up the tents.
I almost forgot to hammer in the pegs.
As Mum rolls out the sleeping bags,
I get back in the car
with my brother and Dad.

In a tiny store,
Dad reads the shopping list:
"We need a box of eggs,
a tin of beans,
and sausages."

Two boxes of eggs.
Three tins of beans.
As Dad looks for sausages,
My brother and I find a bag -
of marshmallows.

Dad returns with a wide smile.
"We need crackers
and chocolate for s'mores."

Arriving back at the campsite,
all of us
begin building a campfire
with logs,
sticks,
and a box of matches.

Dad lights the match
with a SCRATCH!

While Mum and Dad cook dinner,
We run over to the playground
to play with fellow campers.

"Dinner!" Mum calls.
Running towards the campfire,
We smell beans and sausages -
but not marshmallows
or chocolate.

I eat the meal
as it starts to get dark.

Adding more logs,
The campfire burns strongly.

"It's time!" Dad shouts.
We all get excited
As he brings the marshmallows out.

Santa's Arrival

Every Christmas,
many children
try to stay awake -
all looking out
for Santa and Rudolph.

Creeping downstairs
to check the fire isn't burning
within the chimney.

Leaving a mince pie,
a piece of Christmas cake,
and a carrot.

No sign of embers,
and children
They are sent back upstairs to bed.
They might not sleep
straight away,
still trying
to spot Santa -
His sleigh is full of presents.

Children staying awake

on Christmas Eve -
It isn't brand new information.
Children have,
and continue to do it
to this day.

Checking the chimney
several times for embers,
leaving out their stockings
and treats for Father Christmas.

Hephaestus

A deformity -
having been thrown
straight into the ocean.
A course of revenge
against the mother
who gave Hephaestus life.

As the baby grew up
into a craftsman -
a master of fire and forgery,
Much like welders and blacksmiths today.

The baby boy
was now the God of Fire,
always covered in soot and dirt.

Creating jewellery and adornments alike,
even forging
suits of armour -
in preparation
for battles and war.

Timeless is Fire

A thousand years ago,
Humans relied on fire -
for the transformation of materials,
for warmth,
to cook and prepare meals,
to see
when the sun had set.

When cold and darkness
arrive before you know it,
Humans' relationship with flames
has given rise to countless myths
and spiritual healing.

To many cultures,
ash and embers
provide a powerful symbol.

Festive Winter

Cold, cold nights.
Families cuddle up
together by the fire.

Dinner is served,
filling the house
with the aromas of Christmas -
the mint of candy canes,
oranges, and gingerbread.

Christmas cake,
mince pies, and cookies.
Oh, not forgetting
the turkey -
and of course, carrots.
Carrots?

Fire rages,
narrowly missing the stockings.
By the time Santa turns up,
the fire's out.
You begin to feel
the cold of December.

Lights (Still it's Christmas)

Perhaps
They have been left up
right past December,
into the New Year -
past the festive months.
The streetlights continue
to turn off and on.
Still,
some Christmas lights
remain hanging
from roofs and houses.

Place

At the centre of every home,
a fire once burned -
steady and slow.

Tending both bread and prayer,
the heart of the house,
pride of place.

Across centuries,
faiths have crumbled,
been reshaped.

A spark.
A flicker.
Hope ignited -
like a burning flame.

The Knowledge that Grows

The beginning,
middle, and the end.
Decisions are made.
Could you take note
of the consequences?

Regardless,
a new adventure,
a new challenge
within the circle of life.

Simple, healthier changes -
fire burning,
overcoming obstacles.
Experiences make us
grow stronger,
gaining much-needed strength -
all from raging fire.

The Skies (Weather)

In the early hours,
the sun rises,
even though the sky is grey
And the forecast calls for rain.

The wild energy of the weather -
at sunrise,
The skies begin clearing.
Sunshine peeks out
from behind the clouds.

It's clear skies and sunshine.
It may be cold,
But the sun makes it seem warmer.

As day turns to evening,
colder weather
comes knocking after dinner.

The stars burn brightly,
just like the sunshine
high in the sky
around lunchtime.

Secrets of a Stonebake

The stones of a building -
If only they could talk.
They would no doubt have
thousands of stories
from a stone-bake oven.

If bricks in the walls
could only speak,
Perhaps the pizza oven
began its life
in the bakery
of the Great Fire of London.

Returning to the present,
the stone bake oven -
cooks up a masterpiece.

Soon it will produce a pizza
or a loaf of bread -
tasty treats,
baked at home,
not in the local bakery.

A meal for one,
a family gathering
around the table.

Just what,
if possible,
Could the stones
What does an oven reveal?

A Sculpture of Margherita

Flames of a pizza
have nothing to do with the topping.
The actual sculpture
is the pizza base: the dough.

The boat -
The vessel holding the source.
All of the toppings are cooked,
but not beyond charcoal.

The sculpture forms,
rising as the heat absorbs.
The fire's energy
whispers to the cheese,
tomato, and basil.

Put the Fire Out

Fetching buckets of water,
helping to put out
a historical fire.
The burning building -
soon to turn to ash.

Alerting,
calling the fire department.
Engines arrive one
after another.

The building collapsed.
The fire -
The flames have been dampened.
Ashes and cinders
are all that remain
of the buildings.

Baby, Evergreen Dragon

A puff from a hiccup.
Followed by a spark.
Lighting up the sky.
A torch
Showing the way.
In the dark.

An escaping puff of smoke.
The tiny beginnings
Of a fire-breathing dragon.

This dragon isn't supposed to be
to burn down houses.
The baby dragon,
Just wanted to play games.
Constantly,
Looking for fun.

The evergreen dragon,
And it's evergreen scales.
Blushed a shade of red.
When he realised -
He was the cause.

Of a house catching fire.

"I'm so sorry."
Said the dragon.

"I can't control my emotions."

"I haven't even
learnt to fly yet."

Trying to laugh
and not burst into tears.
With a WHOOSH!
A hedge was set ablaze.

"Oops. I'm sorry, everyone"
Wailed the dragon.

He was just a baby.
Learning.
Managing his emotions.

AUTHOR'S NOTE

It's taken a while, but I have, at last, completed the second book in **the Elements in Poetry Series.** The focus is solely on the classic element of fire. Thinking of the classic element of fire, I immediately thought of *Destruction*. Still, while writing the first part of the poetry collection, I began to think about fire burning as a positive force.

Did that take much research? **Yes.**

Did it require some thinking outside of the box? **Yes.**

Are some of the themes a stretch? **Yes.**

I'll let you, the readers, decide on that one.

I have been attempting to edit, illustrate, and proofread specific manuscripts myself, but I still require the assistance of the wonderful proofreader, Loveth E. I am so thankful to work alongside her. Nevertheless, I've recently been purchasing my own ISBN barcodes. This allows me to sell my books at local stallholder events. Especially when writing and publishing at the beginning of the Christmas season. The local community has been very supportive of my writing, and I "couldn't be happier," as they say in Wicked, the musical. In particular, I would like to extend my biggest thanks to the congregation of the Alresford Methodist Church, as well as the staff at Coffee#1 (a local shop), and to the barista at The Town House, another local cafe/restaurant in the area.

I couldn't write this without a huge thank you to my family and friends who have and continue to support me through the ups and downs of a poet and self-published author. I would like to extend a particular thank you to my Mum, brother, and family friend (my Godmother), Chris, who introduced me to stallholding in the first place.

Last but by no means least, thank you for buying and reading my poetry and books. If you haven't read the first book in the Elements in Poetry Series, then please check that out. I wouldn't say you need to read the books in order, but I would recommend it.
Details for all my books are available on my website or on Amazon Worldwide. The easiest method of searching for any of my books is selecting the book category via Amazon and typing in my author's pen name: Margaret Lee Morgan.

Earth, Air, Water & Fire: Classic Elements of Nature (Book 1)

Readers experience an insight into all four, classic elements of nature. Reflecting upon

- The strength of the earth
- The freedom of the wind, the air
- The flow of the river and the storming ocean: water,
- The dark wilds of fire.

Explore a poet's unexpected theming. Allow the four elements to tackle memories, both good and bad, transformations, loss, and renewal.